H ST. IIA S CHURCH TEMPLE SHOLOM ASSEMBLY OF CHRISTIAN CHURCH CHICAGO TEMPLE FIRST UNITED METHODIST CHU
SAINTS EPISCOPAL CHURCH CORPUS CHRISTI CHURCH MOODY MEMORIAL CHURCH ST. PR
EL CHURCH HYDE PARK UNION CHURCH ST. CHRYSOSTOM'S CHURCH ALL SAINTS — ST. A
OCKEFELLER MEMORIAL CHAPEL ST. VIATOR CHURCH THE FUN CHURCH ST. PAUL CHUR
N CHURCH OLIVET BAPTIST CHURCH SEVENTEENTH CHURCH OF CHRIST, SCIENTIST HOLY TRINITY ORTHODOX CATHEDRAL
CHURCH MASJID-E-NOOR ST. BENEDICT'S CHURCH RAINBOW/PUSH UNITY TEMPLE CHICAGO SINAI CONGREGATION GRANV
T. ALPHONSUS CHURCH CHICAGO ILLINOIS TEMPLE FRIENDSHIP ASSEMBLY OF GOD ST. JOSEPH'S UKRAINIAN CATHOLIC CHU
N CHRIST ST. MARY OF PERPETUAL HELP CHURCH VIVEKANANDA TEMPLE EBENEZER LUTHERAN CHURCH HOLY TRINITY PO
E CHURCH ST. JOHN CANTIUS CHURCH NORTH SHORE SEVENTH-DAY ADVENTIST CHURCH FOURTH PRESBYTERIAN CHURCH
ASJID AL-FAATIR CHURCH OF THE LORD JESUS C   HEDWIG CHURCH BAHÁ'Í HOUSE OF W
NTECOSTAL CHURCH KIMBALL AVENUE EVANGEL   VINCENT DE PAUL CHURCH LINCOLN P
TIST CHURCH NORWEGIAN LUTHERAN MEMORIA   HA UKRAINIAN CATHOLIC PARISH QU
OUR ST. MARY OF THE ANGELS CHURCH FIRST   E VIEW PRESBYTERIAN CHURCH ST. I
GELICAL LUTHERAN CHURCH HARE KRISHNA TE   ST. CLEMENT'S CHURCH ALL SAINTS E
POSTLE CHURCH ASSUMPTION CHURCH CHURC   RCH OUR LADY OF MT. CARMEL CHU
TEMPLE OF GREATER CHICAGO METROPOLITAN   N OF ALL SAINTS BASILICA ROCKEFEI
N ST. NICHOLAS CATHEDRAL O'HARE AIRPORT C   RCH BEVERLY UNITARIAN CHURCH OL
ST. JAMES CATHEDRAL THE SALVATION ARMY A   TIST CONGREGATIONAL CHURCH MAS
ST CHURCH ST. MARY OF THE LAKE CHURCH M   LE COMMUNITY CHURCH ST. ALPHON
RCH KAM ISAIAH ISRAEL CONGREGATION MADO   E TEMPLE CHURCH OF GOD IN CHRIST
OUR LORD RECTORY ST. BASIL GREEK ORTHODO   GOD LAKEVIEW MENNONITE CHURCH
NAME CATHEDRAL KINGDOM HALL OF JEHOVA   OLY ANGELS CHURCH MASJID AL-FA
T. SIMEON MIROTOCIVI SERBIAN ORTHODOX CH   TH SIDE UNITED PENTECOSTAL CHU
ROSARY CHURCH ST. STANISLAUS KOSTKA CHU   SOUTH PARK BAPTIST CHURCH NOR
. PATRICK'S CHURCH SHEPHERD'S TEMPLE MISS   RCH OF OUR SAVIOUR ST. MARY OF
IBLY OF CHRISTIAN CHURCH CHICAGO TEMPLE   ST ST. PAUL'S EVANGELICAL LUTHE
RISTI CHURCH MOODY MEMORIAL CHURCH ST.   PLE ST. THOMAS THE APOSTLE CHU
ST. CHRYSOSTOM'S CHURCH ALL SAINTS — ST.   AN CHURCH HINDU TEMPLE OF GREA
RCH THE FUN CHURCH ST. PAUL CHURCH WALI   F THE ASCENSION ST. NICHOLAS CAT
CHURCH OF CHRIST, SCIENTIST HOLY TRINITY ORTHODOX CATHEDRAL OUR LADY OF SORROWS BASILICA ST. JAMES CATHEI
RAINBOW/PUSH UNITY TEMPLE CHICAGO SINAI CONGREGATION GRANVILLE AVENUE UNITED METHODIST CHURCH ST. MAR
FRIENDSHIP ASSEMBLY OF GOD ST. JOSEPH'S UKRAINIAN CATHOLIC CHURCH TRINITY EPISCOPAL CHURCH KAM ISAIAH ISI
H VIVEKANANDA TEMPLE EBENEZER LUTHERAN CHURCH HOLY TRINITY POLISH CHURCH NATIVITY OF OUR LORD RECTORY
ORE SEVENTH-DAY ADVENTIST CHURCH FOURTH PRESBYTERIAN CHURCH ST. MICHAEL'S CHURCH HOLY NAME CATHEDRAL K
ST OF THE APOSTOLIC FAITH ST. HEDWIG CHURCH BAHÁ'Í HOUSE OF WORSHIP HOLY FAMILY CHURCH ST. SIMEON MIROTO
CONGREGATIONAL CHURCH ST. VINCENT DE PAUL CHURCH LINCOLN PARK PRESBYTERIAN CHURCH HOLY ROSARY CHURC

CHICAGO CHURCHES

A PHOTOGRAPHIC ESSAY

CHICAGO CHURCHES

A PHOTOGRAPHIC ESSAY

ELIZABETH JOHNSON

FOR COOKIE NANNY

COPYRIGHT © 1999 BY UPPERCASE BOOKS, INC.
PHOTOGRAPHY COPYRIGHT © 1999 BY ELIZABETH JOHNSON

FIRST EDITION
ISBN 0-9670670-0-6
LIBRARY OF CONGRESS CATALOG CARD NUMBER: 99-90320

PUBLISHED BY UPPERCASE BOOKS, INC.
223 WEST ERIE STREET 4SW CHICAGO ILLINOIS 60610
WWW.UPPERCASEBOOKS.COM

The publisher has made every attempt to contact the original copyright holder of the following works, and grateful acknowledgement is extended to the holders of copyright for their permission to reprint passages. PAGES 24, 89, 117: From *Revised Standard Version of the Bible*, copyright 1946, 1952, 1971 by the Division of Christian Education of the National Council of the Churches of Christ in the USA. Used by permission. PAGE 41: From *The Noble Qur'an, The First American Translation*, trans. Thomas B. Irving. Copyright © 1992, Amana Books. PAGE 54: Reprinted with approval from *Science and Health with Key to the Scriptures* by Mary Baker Eddy. PAGE 71: *The Dhammapada* (author's translation). PAGE 80: From *A Treasury of Jewish Quotations*, by Joseph L. Baron. Reprinted by permission of the publisher, Jason Aronson, Inc., Northvale, NJ © 1985. PAGE 100: Reprinted by permission from *The Bhagavad Gita*, by Eknath Easwaran, founder and director of the Blue Mountain Center of Meditation, copyright 1985. PAGE 128: Reprinted by permission from *Gleanings from the Writings of Bahá'u'lláh*, by Bahá'u'lláh, © 1976 National Spiritual Assembly of the Bahá'ís of the United States.

Although the publisher has made every attempt to ensure the accuracy of information in this book, the publisher assumes no responsibility for errors, inaccuracies, omissions or any other inconsistencies.

A PORTION OF THE PROCEEDS FROM THE SALE OF THIS BOOK WILL BE DONATED TO CHICAGO CHARITABLE AND COMMUNITY ORGANIZATIONS.

TABLE OF CONTENTS

FOREWORD

Chicago was built by people from around the world, drawn here by the opportunity to work for a better life. They carried their faiths with them, and our city was soon a mosaic of beliefs as well as languages and customs.

Proud of their origins, members of each community pooled their resources and erected monuments to their faiths. These churches, synagogues, temples and places of worship became civic landmarks and unique expressions of the culture, tradition and beliefs of each group. They also helped to define the unique character of Chicago, and to symbolize the commitment our immigrants were making to their new home.

The history of Chicago cannot be told without speaking at length about the role that the place of worship has played in the daily lives of our communities. I am pleased to introduce *Chicago Churches: A Photographic Essay*, and am certain that this book will do much to inform and enlighten you as to the beauty, the history and the importance of churches in Chicago.

MAYOR

CHICAGO CHURCHES

A PHOTOGRAPHIC ESSAY

A church, by its most limited meaning, is defined as a building in which Christians meet for religious worship. In a broader sense though, a church can be seen as any sacred place — any building, or structure, or space with the capacity to hold spiritual meaning. It is a place, regardless of its appearance, that a community holds in reverence. It is in this spirit that you will find synagogues, mosques, and other houses of worship in this essay as well. Be they stone or wood, glorious or quiet, majestic or humble, our churches are reflections of us. A church, as we are commonly taught, is not as much the building itself, but the collective spirit of the people who gather within it. And in that spirit people have the opportunity to see themselves and their communities in a different way. Look through and beyond the following images to see more than the physical structures. Look, and you will see yourself and those around you. You will see, too, that our hopes and dreams share a common thread of spirit, and goodness, and faith.

PLATE I

ST. ALPHONSUS CHURCH   2950 North Southport Avenue, Chicago   ROMAN CATHOLIC

PLATE ²

HOLY TRINITY POLISH CHURCH   1120 North Noble Street, Chicago   ROMAN CATHOLIC

PLATE³

METROPOLITAN MISSIONARY BAPTIST CHURCH   2151 West Washington Boulevard, Chicago   BAPTIST

PLATE⁴

SEVENTEENTH CHURCH OF CHRIST, SCIENTIST   55 East Wacker Drive, Chicago   CHRISTIAN SCIENCE

PLATE⁵

ST. NICHOLAS CATHEDRAL   2238 West Rice Street, Chicago   UKRAINIAN CATHOLIC

SUMMERDALE COMMUNITY CHURCH   1700 West Farragut Avenue, Chicago   UNITED CHURCH OF CHRIST

 PLATE 7

MOODY MEMORIAL CHURCH   1609 North LaSalle Drive, Chicago   NONDENOMINATIONAL

PLATE 8

TEMPLE SHOLOM   3480 North Lake Shore Drive, Chicago   REFORM JUDAISM

PLATE 9

FIRST BAPTIST CONGREGATIONAL CHURCH   60 North Ashland Avenue, Chicago   BAPTIST

"Faith is the assurance
of things hoped for,
the conviction
of things not seen."

CHRISTIANITY | Bible, Hebrews, 11.1

PLATE 10

PLATE II

OLD ST. PATRICK'S CHURCH   140 South Desplaines Street, Chicago   ROMAN CATHOLIC

PLATE 12

ANNUNCIATION CATHEDRAL   1017 North LaSalle Drive, Chicago   GREEK ORTHODOX

PLATE [13]

MORGAN PARK CHURCH OF GOD   11153 South Hoyne Avenue, Chicago   CHURCH OF GOD (ANDERSON, IN)

PLATE 14

ST. JAMES CATHEDRAL   65 East Huron Street, Chicago   EPISCOPAL

KINGDOM HALL OF JEHOVAH'S WITNESSES   5008 West Diversey Avenue, Chicago   JEHOVAH'S WITNESSES

ST. VIATOR CHURCH   4170 West Addison Street, Chicago   ROMAN CATHOLIC

PLATE [17]

BEVERLY UNITARIAN CHURCH   10244 South Longwood Drive, Chicago   UNITARIAN UNIVERSALIST

PLATE 18

ST. PAUL CHURCH   2234 South Hoyne Avenue, Chicago   ROMAN CATHOLIC

PLATE 19

ASSEMBLY OF CHRISTIAN CHURCH   2840 West Logan Boulevard, Chicago   PENTECOSTAL

PLATE²⁰

PLATE ²⁰

HINDU TEMPLE OF GREATER CHICAGO   10915 Lemont Road, Lemont   HINDU

| PLATE 21 |

ST. PROCOPIUS CHURCH   1641 South Allport Street, Chicago   ROMAN CATHOLIC

PLATE 22

ST. THOMAS THE APOSTLE CHURCH   5472 South Kimbark Avenue, Chicago   ROMAN CATHOLIC

NORTH SIDE UNITED PENTECOSTAL CHURCH   1527 West Edgewater Avenue, Chicago   PENTECOSTAL

"Those who act kindly
in this world
will have kindness."

ISLAM │ Qur'an, 39.10

PLATE²⁴

PLATE ²⁴

ST. MARY OF THE ANGELS CHURCH   1850 North Hermitage Avenue, Chicago   ROMAN CATHOLIC

PLATE 25

CHURCH OF THE ATONEMENT   5749 North Kenmore Avenue, Chicago   EPISCOPAL

PLATE 26

FIRST ST. PAUL'S EVANGELICAL LUTHERAN CHURCH   1301 North LaSalle Drive, Chicago   LUTHERAN

PLATE 27

ST. CHRYSOSTOM'S CHURCH   1424 North Dearborn Parkway, Chicago   EPISCOPAL

PLATE 28

ST. JOSEPH'S UKRAINIAN CATHOLIC CHURCH   5000 North Cumberland Avenue, Chicago   UKRAINIAN CATHOLIC

PLATE[29]

LAKEVIEW MENNONITE CHURCH   2812 North Lincoln Avenue, Chicago   MENNONITE

PLATE 30

ST. JOHN CANTIUS CHURCH   825 North Carpenter Street, Chicago   ROMAN CATHOLIC

PLATE 31

UNITY TEMPLE   875 West Lake Street, Oak Park   UNITARIAN UNIVERSALIST

PLATE 32

ST. SIMEON MIROTOCIVI SERBIAN ORTHODOX CHURCH   3737 East 114ᵀᴴ Street, Chicago   SERBIAN ORTHODOX

PLATE 33

OUR LADY OF MT. CARMEL CHURCH   690 West Belmont Avenue, Chicago   ROMAN CATHOLIC

PLATE 34

SOUTH PARK BAPTIST CHURCH 　　 3722 South Dr. Martin Luther King Jr. Drive, Chicago 　　 BAPTIST

PLATE 35

OUR LADY OF LOURDES CHURCH   4640 North Ashland Avenue, Chicago   ROMAN CATHOLIC

"Spirit is the life, substance, and continuity of all things."

CHRISTIAN SCIENCE | Science and Health, *124*

PLATE³⁶

CHURCH OF THE SPIRIT   2651 North Central Park Avenue, Chicago   SPIRITUALIST

PLATE 37

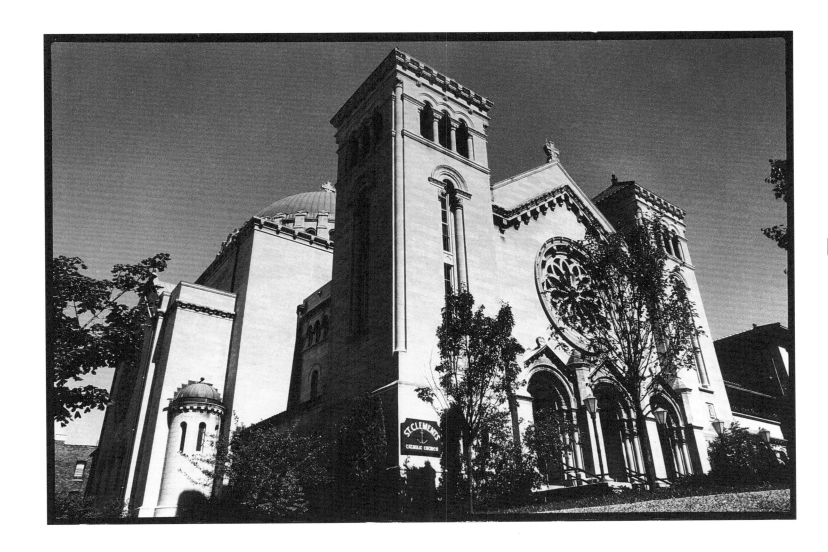

ST. CLEMENT'S CHURCH   646 West Deming Place, Chicago   ROMAN CATHOLIC

PLATE³⁸

HOLY TRINITY ORTHODOX CATHEDRAL   1121 North Leavitt Street, Chicago   ORTHODOX

PLATE³⁹

CHICAGO TEMPLE FIRST UNITED METHODIST CHURCH   77 West Washington Street, Chicago   UNITED METHODIST

PLATE 40

BAHÁ'Í HOUSE OF WORSHIP   100 Linden Avenue, Wilmette   BAHÁ'Í FAITH

LINCOLN PARK PRESBYTERIAN CHURCH   600 West Fullerton Parkway, Chicago   PRESBYTERIAN

כי ביתי בית תפלה
יקרא לכל העמים

CHICAGO SINAI CONGREGATION   15 West Delaware Place, Chicago   REFORM JUDAISM

PLATE⁴³

ST. STANISLAUS KOSTKA CHURCH   1327 North Noble Street, Chicago   ROMAN CATHOLIC

PLATE⁴⁴

VIVEKANANDA TEMPLE   5423 South Hyde Park Boulevard, Chicago   VEDANTA SOCIETY

PLATE 45

OUR LADY OF SORROWS BASILICA   3121 West Jackson Boulevard, Chicago   ROMAN CATHOLIC

PLATE 46

CHURCH OF OUR SAVIOUR   530 West Fullerton Parkway, Chicago   EPISCOPAL

| PLATE⁴⁷ |

THE FUN CHURCH   1905 West Schiller Street, Chicago   NONDENOMINATIONAL

ST. VINCENT DE PAUL CHURCH   1010 West Webster Avenue, Chicago   ROMAN CATHOLIC

NORTH SHORE SEVENTH-DAY ADVENTIST CHURCH   5220 North California Avenue, Chicago   SEVENTH-DAY ADVENTIST

"Let a man subdue
anger by love,
let him conquer evil by good;
let him overcome
greed by giving
and the liar by truth."

BUDDHISM | Dhammapada, 223

PLATE 50

ST. MICHAEL'S CHURCH   1633 North Cleveland Avenue, Chicago   ROMAN CATHOLIC

CHURCH OF THE ASCENSION   1133 North LaSalle Drive, Chicago   EPISCOPAL

PLATE⁵²

MASJID AL-FAATIR   1200 East 47ᵀᴴ Street, Chicago   ISLAMIC

PLATE⁵³

THE SALVATION ARMY   1415 West Belmont Avenue, Chicago   SALVATION ARMY

ST. IGNATIUS CHURCH   6559 North Glenwood Avenue, Chicago   ROMAN CATHOLIC

PLATE⁵⁵

FOURTH PRESBYTERIAN CHURCH 866 North Michigan Avenue, Chicago PRESBYTERIAN

PLATE 56

NOTRE DAME DE CHICAGO CHURCH   1336 West Flournoy Street, Chicago   ROMAN CATHOLIC

FRIENDSHIP ASSEMBLY OF GOD   1400 West Bryn Mawr Avenue, Chicago   ASSEMBLIES OF GOD

"All men are responsible for one another."

JUDAISM | Talmud, Sanhedrin *27b*

PLATE 58

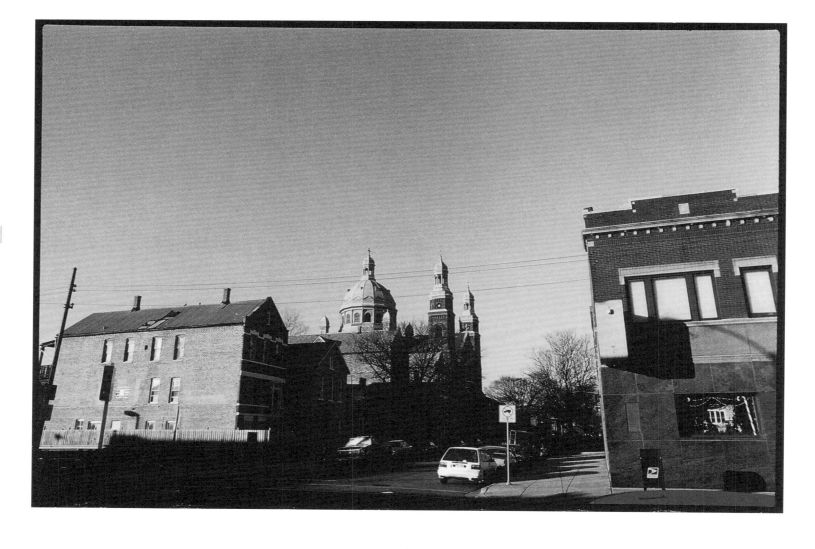

ST. MARY OF PERPETUAL HELP CHURCH   1035 West 32ND Street, Chicago   ROMAN CATHOLIC

| PLATE 59 |

QUINN CHAPEL A.M.E. CHURCH   2401 South Wabash Avenue, Chicago   AFRICAN METHODIST EPISCOPAL

PLATE 60

CHURCH OF THE LORD JESUS CHRIST OF THE APOSTOLIC FAITH   3202 West Ogden Avenue, Chicago   APOSTOLIC

PLATE 61

ST. MATTHEW LUTHERAN CHURCH   2108 West 21ˢᵀ Street, Chicago   LUTHERAN

PLATE 62

ST. PHILIP NERI CHURCH   2132 East 72ND Street, Chicago   ROMAN CATHOLIC

PLATE 63

CHICAGO ILLINOIS TEMPLE   4151 West Lake Avenue, Glenview   THE CHURCH OF JESUS CHRIST OF LATTER-DAY SAINTS

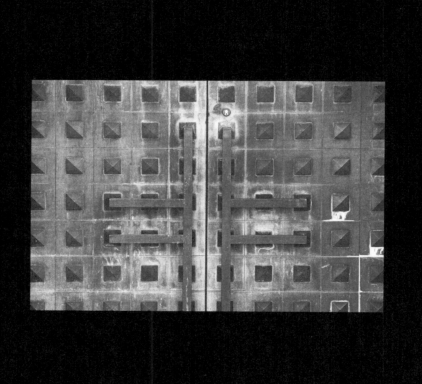

"Give, and it will
be given to you...
for the measure you give
will be the measure
you get back."

CHRISTIANITY | Bible, Luke, 6.38

PLATE⁶⁴

LAKE VIEW PRESBYTERIAN CHURCH   716 West Addison Street, Chicago   PRESBYTERIAN

PLATE 65

MADONNA DELLA STRADA CHAPEL   6525 North Sheridan Road, Chicago   ROMAN CATHOLIC

PLATE 66

SHEPHERD'S TEMPLE MISSIONARY BAPTIST CHURCH   3411 West Douglas Boulevard, Chicago   BAPTIST

PLATE 67

QUEEN OF ALL SAINTS BASILICA   6280 North Sauganash Avenue, Chicago   ROMAN CATHOLIC

PLATE 68

RAINBOW/PUSH   930 East 50ᵀᴴ Street, Chicago   BAPTIST

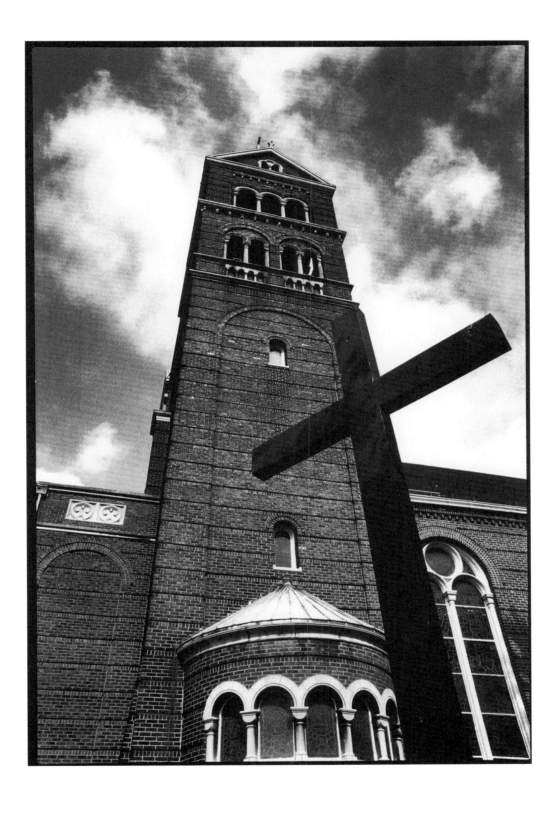

PLATE 69

ALL SAINTS — ST. ANTHONY CHURCH   518 West 28ᵀᴴ Place, Chicago   ROMAN CATHOLIC

PLATE⁷⁰

MIDWEST BUDDHIST TEMPLE   435 West Menomonee Street, Chicago   BUDDHIST

PLATE 71

CORPUS CHRISTI CHURCH   4920 South Dr. Martin Luther King Jr. Drive, Chicago   ROMAN CATHOLIC

PLATE 72

HOLY NAME CATHEDRAL   735 North State Street, Chicago   ROMAN CATHOLIC

| PLATE 73 |

ST. BASIL GREEK ORTHODOX CHURCH   733 South Ashland Avenue, Chicago   GREEK ORTHODOX

"I look upon
     all creatures equally;
none are less dear to me
     and none more dear."

HINDUISM | Bhagavad Gita, 9.29

PLATE 74

PLATE 75

ST. ITA'S CHURCH   5500 North Broadway Street, Chicago   ROMAN CATHOLIC

PLATE ⁷⁶

ROCKEFELLER MEMORIAL CHAPEL   5850 South Woodlawn Avenue, Chicago   INTERDENOMINATIONAL

| PLATE⁷⁷ |

MASJID-E-NOOR   6151 North Greenview Avenue, Chicago   ISLAMIC

PLATE 78

NATIVITY OF OUR LORD RECTORY   653 West 37ᵀᴴ Street, Chicago   ROMAN CATHOLIC

PLATE 79

HYDE PARK UNION CHURCH   5600 South Woodlawn Avenue, Chicago   UNITED CHURCH OF CHRIST

PLATE 80

ST. MARY OF THE LAKE CHURCH   4200 North Sheridan Road, Chicago   ROMAN CATHOLIC

PLATE 81

PARADISE TEMPLE CHURCH OF GOD IN CHRIST   11445 South Forest Avenue, Chicago   CHURCH OF GOD IN CHRIST

PLATE 82

WALLS MEMORIAL C.M.E. CHURCH   200 South Sacramento Boulevard, Chicago   CHRISTIAN METHODIST EPISCOPAL

PLATE 83

HOLY ROSARY CHURCH   11300 South Dr. Martin Luther King Jr. Drive, Chicago   ROMAN CATHOLIC

PLATE 84

EBENEZER LUTHERAN CHURCH   1650 West Foster Avenue, Chicago   LUTHERAN

| PLATE ⁸⁵ |

HARE KRISHNA TEMPLE   1716 West Lunt Avenue, Chicago   INTERNATIONAL SOCIETY FOR KRISHNA CONSCIOUSNESS

KAM ISAIAH ISRAEL CONGREGATION   1100 East Hyde Park Boulevard, Chicago   REFORM JUDAISM

PLATE 87

ALL SAINTS EPISCOPAL CHURCH   4550 North Hermitage Avenue, Chicago   EPISCOPAL

"You shall love
your neighbor
as yourself."

CHRISTIANITY AND JUDAISM | Bible, Leviticus 19.18

PLATE 88

PLATE 89

SECOND PRESBYTERIAN CHURCH   1936 South Michigan Avenue, Chicago   PRESBYTERIAN

PLATE 90

ST. BENEDICT'S CHURCH   2201 West Irving Park Road, Chicago   ROMAN CATHOLIC

PLATE 91

STS. VOLODYMYR AND OLHA UKRAINIAN CATHOLIC PARISH   739 North Oakley Boulevard, Chicago   UKRAINIAN CATHOLIC

OLIVET BAPTIST CHURCH   3101 South Dr. Martin Luther King Jr. Drive, Chicago   BAPTIST

| PLATE 93 |

ST. HEDWIG CHURCH   2100 West Webster Avenue, Chicago   ROMAN CATHOLIC

PLATE 94

HOLY FAMILY CHURCH   1080 West Roosevelt Road, Chicago   ROMAN CATHOLIC

PLATE 95

QUANG MINH TEMPLE   4429 North Damen Avenue, Chicago   BUDDHIST

GRANVILLE AVENUE UNITED METHODIST CHURCH   1307 West Granville Avenue, Chicago   UNITED METHODIST

PLATE 97

FIRST UNITARIAN CHURCH OF CHICAGO   5650 South Woodlawn Avenue, Chicago   UNITARIAN UNIVERSALIST

"So powerful
        is the light of unity
that it can illuminate
        the whole earth."

BAHÁ'Í FAITH | Gleanings from the Writings of Bahá'u'lláh

PLATE 98

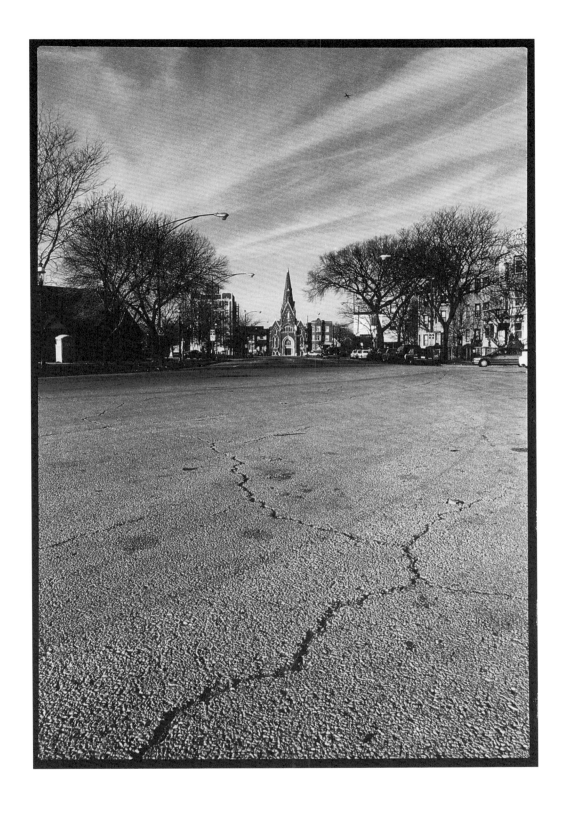

PLATE 99

NORWEGIAN LUTHERAN MEMORIAL CHURCH   2614 North Kedzie Avenue, Chicago   LUTHERAN

PLATE 100

ASSUMPTION CHURCH   323 West Illinois Street, Chicago   ROMAN CATHOLIC

LIST OF PLATES *(alphabetically by church)*

ACKNOWLEDGEMENTS

I WOULD LIKE TO OFFER MY MOST SINCERE THANKS TO EVERYONE WHO HAS HELPED MAKE THIS BOOK POSSIBLE. TO BROCK; your thoughtful and constant critique, business guidance, and support allowed me to take this project from idea to reality. TO EVERYONE AT PIVOT DESIGN; thank you for your thoughts, support, and continuing inspiration. TO THE HONORABLE MAYOR RICHARD M. DALEY; your dedication to the bringing together of Chicago's communities is shown in many ways, and your contribution truly helped to make this book complete. TO MICHAEL C. NOBLE; thank you for your professional guidance and insight. TO PEGGY; thank you for your polishing. TO COOKIE PAPA; your passion and expertise on the subject that you love has made me strive to make this book all that it could be. TO DR. AMBERG; your encouragement and support pushed me to believe that accomplishing this goal would be as simple, and as difficult, as taking the chance. AND TO MY PARENTS; thank you for always giving of yourselves, for always standing by me, and for believing in one of my many, many dreams. —LIZ

COLOPHON

Photography and design by Elizabeth Johnson. The first edition of *Chicago Churches: A Photographic Essay* was printed on NPI Woodfree, 180 gsm, acid-free uncoated paper. The layout of the book was composed using Quark X-Press and Adobe Illustrator with all images separated as individually adjusted metallic tritones using Adobe Photoshop. The text was set in the typefaces Goudy Old Style and Franklin Gothic from Adobe Systems. Photographic prints scanned by Image Studio, Ltd. Printed and bound in China by Palace Press, International.

ABOUT FREDERIC W. GOUDY; The typeface Goudy Old Style was designed by Frederic W. Goudy (1865-1947). A master of typography as well as book design, Goudy brought inspired excellence to both. His passion for the letterform began at a young age. An anecdote tells that while growing up as a child in Bloomington, Illinois, Goudy cut over three thousand letters out of colored paper, turning his church's walls into a multi-colored display of Biblical passages.

RCH OF OUR SAVIOUR ST. MARY OF THE ANGELS CHURCH FIRST UNITARIAN CHURCH OF CHICAGO LAKE VIEW PRESBYTERI
ST ST. PAUL'S EVANGELICAL LUTHERAN CHURCH HARE KRISHNA TEMPLE OUR LADY OF LOURDES CHURCH ST. CLEMENT'S CH
ST. THOMAS THE APOSTLE CHURCH ASSUMPTION CHURCH CHURCH OF THE SPIRIT ST. PHILIP NERI CHURCH OUR LADY OF
N CHURCH HINDU TEMPLE OF GREATER CHICAGO METROPOLITAN MISSIONARY BAPTIST CHURCH QUEEN OF ALL SAINTS B
RCH OF THE ASCENSION ST. NICHOLAS CATHEDRAL O'HARE AIRPORT CHAPEL ST. MATTHEW LUTHERAN CHURCH BEVERLY
Y OF SORROWS BASILICA ST. JAMES CATHEDRAL THE SALVATION ARMY ANNUNCIATION CATHEDRAL FIRST BAPTIST CONGRE
NUE UNITED METHODIST CHURCH ST. MARY OF THE LAKE CHURCH MIDWEST BUDDHIST TEMPLE SUMMERDALE COMMUNITY
NITY EPISCOPAL CHURCH KAM ISAIAH ISRAEL CONGREGATION MADONNA DELLA STRADA CHAPEL PARADISE TEMPLE CHURCH
RCH NATIVITY OF OUR LORD RECTORY ST. BASIL GREEK ORTHODOX CHURCH MORGAN PARK CHURCH OF GOD LAKEVIEW M
HAEL'S CHURCH HOLY NAME CATHEDRAL KINGDOM HALL OF JEHOVAH'S WITNESSES ST. IGNATIUS CHURCH HOLY ANGELS C
P HOLY FAMILY CHURCH ST. SIMEON MIROTOCIVI SERBIAN ORTHODOX CHURCH CHURCH OF THE ATONEMENT NORTH SIDE U
SBYTERIAN CHURCH HOLY ROSARY CHURCH ST. STANISLAUS KOSTKA CHURCH NOTRE DAME DE CHICAGO CHURCH SOUTH
PEL A.M.E. CHURCH OLD ST. PATRICK'S CHURCH SHEPHERD'S TEMPLE MISSIONARY BAPTIST CHURCH CHURCH CHURCH OF
RCH TEMPLE SHOLOM ASSEMBLY OF CHRISTIAN CHURCH CHICAGO TEMPLE FIRST UNITED METHODIST CHURCH FIRST ST. PAU
AL CHURCH CORPUS CHRISTI CHURCH MOODY MEMORIAL CHURCH ST. PROCOPIUS CHURCH QUANG MINH TEMPLE ST. THO
E PARK UNION CHURCH ST. CHRYSOSTOM'S CHURCH ALL SAINTS — ST. ANTHONY CHURCH SECOND PRESBYTERIAN CHUR
ORIAL CHAPEL ST. VIATOR CHURCH THE FUN CHURCH ST. PAUL CHURCH WALLS MEMORIAL C.M.E. CHURCH CHURCH OF THE
TIST CHURCH SEVENTEENTH CHURCH OF CHRIST, SCIENTIST HOLY TRINITY ORTHODOX CATHEDRAL OUR LADY OF SORROWS
DOR ST. BENEDICT'S CHURCH RAINBOW/PUSH UNITY TEMPLE CHICAGO SINAI CONGREGATION GRANVILLE AVENUE UNITED
RCH CHICAGO ILLINOIS TEMPLE FRIENDSHIP ASSEMBLY OF GOD ST. JOSEPH'S UKRAINIAN CATHOLIC CHURCH TRINITY EPISC
Y OF PERPETUAL HELP CHURCH VIVEKANANDA TEMPLE EBENEZER LUTHERAN CHURCH HOLY TRINITY POLISH CHURCH NAT
N CANTIUS CHURCH NORTH SHORE SEVENTH-DAY ADVENTIST CHURCH FOURTH PRESBYTERIAN CHURCH ST. MICHAEL'S CHU
RCH OF THE LORD JESUS CHRIST OF THE APOSTOLIC FAITH ST. HEDWIG CHURCH BAHÁ'Í HOUSE OF WORSHIP HOLY FAMILY C
BALL AVENUE EVANGELICAL CONGREGATIONAL CHURCH ST. VINCENT DE PAUL CHURCH LINCOLN PARK PRESBYTERIAN CHU
N LUTHERAN MEMORIAL CHURCH STS. VOLODYMYR AND OLHA UKRAINIAN CATHOLIC PARISH QUINN CHAPEL A.M.E. CHURC
ELS CHURCH FIRST UNITARIAN CHURCH OF CHICAGO LAKE VIEW PRESBYTERIAN CHURCH ST. ITA'S CHURCH TEMPLE SHOL
RCH HARE KRISHNA TEMPLE OUR LADY OF LOURDES CHURCH ST. CLEMENT'S CHURCH ALL SAINTS EPISCOPAL CHURCH
MPTION CHURCH CHURCH OF THE SPIRIT ST. PHILIP NERI CHURCH OUR LADY OF MT. CARMEL CHURCH HYDE PARK UNION
AGO METROPOLITAN MISSIONARY BAPTIST CHURCH QUEEN OF ALL SAINTS BASILICA ROCKEFELLER MEMORIAL CHAPEL ST. V
O'HARE AIRPORT CHAPEL ST. MATTHEW LUTHERAN CHURCH BEVERLY UNITARIAN CHURCH OLIVET BAPTIST CHURCH SEVI
SALVATION ARMY ANNUNCIATION CATHEDRAL FIRST BAPTIST CONGREGATIONAL CHURCH MASJID-E-NOOR ST. BENEDICT'S
LAKE CHURCH MIDWEST BUDDHIST TEMPLE SUMMERDALE COMMUNITY CHURCH ST. ALPHONSUS CHURCH CHICAGO ILLINO
GREGATION MADONNA DELLA STRADA CHAPEL PARADISE TEMPLE CHURCH OF GOD IN CHRIST ST. MARY OF PERPETUAL HE
L GREEK ORTHODOX CHURCH MORGAN PARK CHURCH OF GOD LAKEVIEW MENNONITE CHURCH ST. JOHN CANTIUS CHURCH
HALL OF JEHOVAH'S WITNESSES ST. IGNATIUS CHURCH HOLY ANGELS CHURCH MASJID AL-FAATIR CHURCH OF THE LORD
IAN ORTHODOX CHURCH CHURCH OF THE ATONEMENT NORTH SIDE UNITED PENTECOSTAL CHURCH KIMBALL AVENUE EVA